Date: 4/12/11

BATS SET I

FISHERMAN BATS

Tamara L. Britton
ABDO Publishing Company

Published by ABDO Publishing Company, 8000 West 78th Street, Edina, Minnesota
55439. Copyright © 2011 by Abdo Consulting Group, Inc. International copyrights
reserved in all countries. No part of this book may be reproduced in any form without
written permission from the publisher. The Checkerboard Library™ is a trademark and
logo of ABDO Publishing Company.

Printed in the United States of America, North Mankato, Minnesota.
042010
092010

♻ PRINTED ON RECYCLED PAPER

Cover Photo: © Merlin D. Tuttle, Bat Conservation International, www.batcon.org
Interior Photos: Alamy pp. 5, 9; Animals Animals p. 13; Getty Images p. 17;
    © Merlin D. Tuttle, Bat Conservation International, www.batcon.org pp. 11, 18, 19, 21

Editor: BreAnn Rumsch
Art Direction & Cover Design: Neil Klinepier

Library of Congress Cataloging-in-Publication Data

Britton, Tamara L., 1963-
  Fisherman bats / Tamara L. Britton.
      p. cm. -- (Bats)
  Includes bibliographical references and index.
  ISBN 978-1-61613-391-7
  1. Noctilio--Juvenile literature. I. Title.
  QL737.C56B75 2011
  599.4--dc22
                                    2010009359

CONTENTS

FISHERMAN BATS

Heading

Introduction→ Fisherman bats belong to the family **Noctilionidae**. In this family, two species are fisherman bats. They are the greater and lesser fisherman bats. There are more than 1,100 species of bats in the world!

Bats are mammals. One-quarter of all mammals are bats. Like other mammals, mother bats give birth to live babies. They also produce milk to feed their young. But bats can do something no other mammal can do. They can fly!

Some people are afraid of bats. But bats are helpful. They eat millions of insect pests every year. Bold Face type← They also help **pollinate** plants. And, bats plant trees by scattering fruit seeds as they fly. These creatures are a valuable part of their ecosystem.

4

Like all bats, fisherman bats are members of the order Chiroptera. This Greek word means "hand wing." Bats have hands that are also wings!

WHERE THEY'RE FOUND

Bats can be found all around the world. They live everywhere except Antarctica, the polar regions, and a few ocean islands. Most bats live in places that have a **tropical** climate.

Fisherman bats live in North, Central, and South America. They can be found from southern Mexico to northern Argentina to southeastern Brazil. Because of their range, fisherman bats are called **New World** bats.

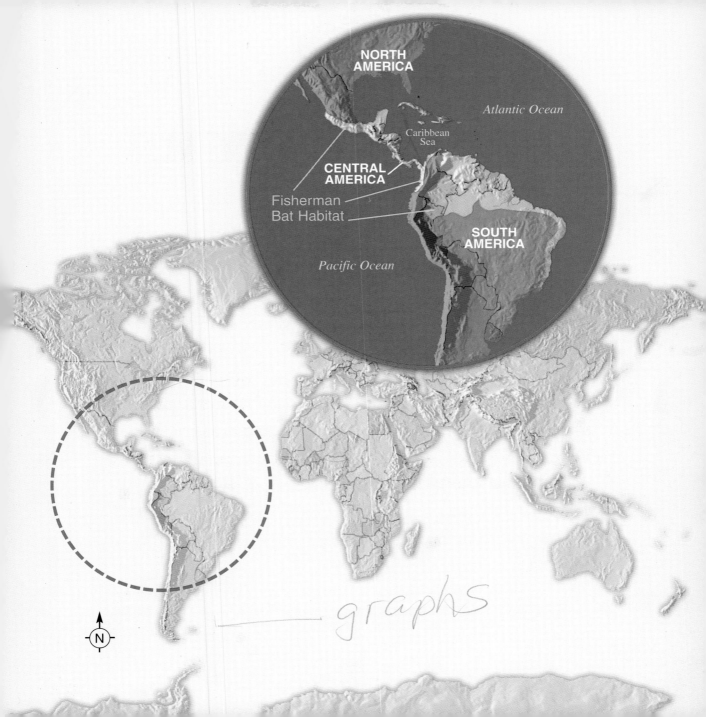

NORTH
AMERICA

Atlantic Ocean

Caribbean
Sea

CENTRAL
AMERICA

Fisherman
Bat Habitat

SOUTH
AMERICA

Pacific Ocean

graphs

N

WHERE THEY LIVE

Fisherman bats hunt fish. So, they live near streams, rivers, lakes, and oceans. Unlike most bats, fisherman bats can swim. They can also take flight from the water's surface. And sometimes, they use their wings as oars!

When they are not hunting, fisherman bats rest at home. They **roost** in caves, hollow trees, and cracks in rocks.

Fisherman bats live in colonies of up to 30 bats. So many bats in one place creates a strong smell. Fisherman bat roosts can often be found because of this!

Long, narrow wings make flying fast over open water easy for fisherman bats.

Did you know facts

8

To **roost**, a bat hangs upside down by its feet. Each foot has five toes with sharp, curved claws. The bat grabs onto the roost with its toes. When it relaxes, a **tendon** in each foot causes the claws to close and grip the roosting site.

SIZES

Bats come in many different sizes. The Malayan flying fox is the world's largest bat. It can grow more than 16 inches (40 cm) long. Its **wingspan** reaches more than 5 feet (1.5 m)!

The Kitti's hog-nosed bat is very tiny. It grows to just 1 inch (2.5 cm) long. That is about the size of a large bumblebee! This small bat has a wingspan of 6 inches (15 cm).

Fisherman bats are medium-sized bats. Greater fisherman bats are 4 to 5 inches (10 to 13 cm) long. They have a wingspan of about 1.5 feet (0.5 m). Males weigh 2.75 ounces (78 g) and females weigh 2.12 ounces (60 g).

Lesser fisherman bats grow 2.2 to 3.4 inches (5.7 to 8.5 cm) long. They weigh 0.6 to 1.5 ounces (18 to 44 g).

The fisherman bat's stretchy cheeks make its lips droop like a bulldog's. So, these bats are also called bulldog bats.

SHAPES

The fisherman bat has a round head. Its big ears are slender and pointed. The bat's face features a pointed snout and large lips. Stretchy cheeks create pouches so the bat can hold food in its mouth.

The fisherman bat's two arms support long, narrow wings. Each arm has a hand with four fingers and a thumb. Black, elastic wing **membranes** stretch between the bat's fingers, body, and legs. They also attach the legs to the tail, forming a tail pouch.

The fisherman bat has short, water-repellent fur. Greater fisherman bat males are pale to dark orange on top. The females are brown to grayish brown. Both males and females have whitish or

bright orange bellies. Lesser fisherman bat males
are red on top with gray brown or yellow
undersides. The females are brown on top.

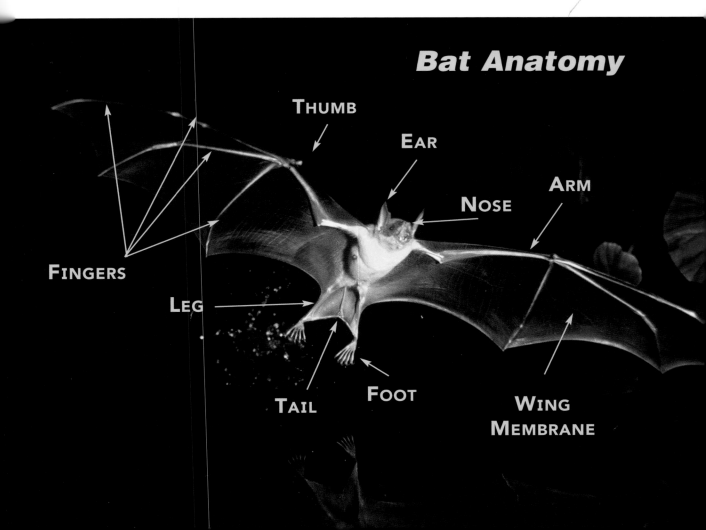

Bat Anatomy

THUMB

EAR

NOSE

ARM

FINGERS

LEG

TAIL

FOOT

WING
MEMBRANE

SENSES

Fisherman bats have five senses, just like you! They can see, hear, smell, taste, and feel. In addition, these bats have a sense called echolocation. This is how these **nocturnal** bats "see" in the dark.

To echolocate, the bats make high-pitched sounds from their throats or noses. These go out and bounce off objects such as trees, buildings, or insects.

The sounds return to the bats as echoes. The bats catch the echoes in their ears. The echoes tell the bats the size and location of the objects. They also tell the bats how big the objects are. Bats use this information to fly safely, find food, and avoid danger.

To catch fish, fisherman bats echolocate over water. Swimming fish make ripples on the water. The bats recognize the echoes these ripples make. They tell the bats where the fish are and how fast they are swimming. This makes it easy for the bats to swoop down and grab some dinner!

Sound wave sent out by bat

Echo wave received by bat

sidebars

DEFENSE

Other animals need to eat dinner, too. Bats make good meals for cats, dogs, raccoons, and skunks. Owls, hawks, falcons, snakes, and large frogs also like to eat bats. Large spiders devour bats that get caught in their webs. And, some bats feast on other bats!

A bat's best defense against these predators is to fly away. The fisherman bat uses its long wings to fly away fast.

Since most bats are **nocturnal**, they hunt at night. This helps them avoid predators that hunt by day. During the day, bats **roost** in safe, dark places. Their dark-colored fur helps them hide in their special roosting spots.

Fisherman bats are skilled nocturnal hunters. They can eat 30 to 40 fish in a single night!

FOOD

As their name suggests, fisherman bats eat fish. Greater fisherman bats also eat fiddler crabs. Lesser fisherman bats eat fish, too. But most of their diet consists of insects. They eat winged ants, crickets, beetles, and stink bugs.

When fishing, these bats fly 1.5 to 4 inches (4 to 10 cm) above the

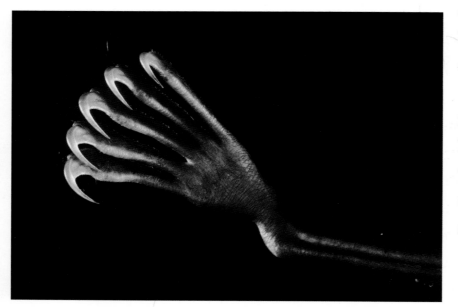

The greater fisherman bat's feet are adapted for grabbing and holding fish. They are wide and flat with long, hooked claws.

Sometimes, fisherman bats do not use echolocation to find food as they fly along. Instead, they rake their feet through water where they know fish like to swim!

water's surface. They use echolocation to listen for echoes from swimming fish. When the bats find a fish, they extend their legs to the water's surface.

The flying bats rake their large feet through the water. Then they use their sharp, curved claws to snatch up the fish! Fisherman bats can eat their food in flight. Or, they may carry it in their cheek pouches to eat back at the **roost**.

BABIES

Fisherman bats usually breed once or twice a year. Each time, the female gives birth to a single baby. The baby bat is called a pup.

When giving birth, the mother bat hangs right side up by her thumbs. She catches her newborn in her tail pouch. Then, the pup climbs up on its mother's chest and begins to nurse.

Newborn pups are very big. At birth, they often weigh 25 percent of their mother's weight. Baby bats can drink their weight in milk every day!

The mother bat needs a lot of energy to produce this much milk. So, she must leave the **roost** to hunt. At first, the mother bat takes her pup along. Later, the pup stays behind in the roost. When the mother returns, she finds her pup by its special smell and squeak sound. The mother bat is careful with her energy and milk resources and feeds only her pup.

When the pup is about one month old, it begins learning to fly. When a pup matures, it can leave the **roost** to find its own food. Then, it looks for a mate and has pups of its own. In this way, the fisherman bat takes its place in its ecosystem.

A fisherman bat mother gives birth during the wet season. At that time of year, there is enough food available for the pup's survival.

captions

GLOSSARY

membrane - a thin, easily bent layer of animal tissue.

New World - all the continents of the western half of Earth.

Noctilionidae (nahk-tihl-ee-AHN-uh-dee) - the scientific name for the family of fish-eating bats.

nocturnal - active at night.

pollinate - when birds, insects, or winds transfer pollen from one flower or plant to another.

roost - to perch or settle down to rest. A roost is a place, such as a cave or a tree, where animals rest.

tendon - a band of tough fibers that joins a muscle to another body part, such as a bone.

tropical - having a climate in which there is no frost and plants can grow all year long.

wingspan - the distance from one wing tip to the other when the wings are spread.

WEB SITES

To learn more about fisherman bats, visit ABDO Publishing Company on the World Wide Web at **www.abdopublishing.com**. Web sites about fisherman bats are featured on our Book Links page. These links are routinely monitored and updated to provide the most current information available.

INDEX